EiM Anthology with Mark Grist

VOICES

2024

Billson International Ltd.

Published by
Billson International Ltd
Unit 205,Unit C, 2/F, Kwong On Bank Mongkok Branch Building
728-730 Nathan Road
Mong Kok
Hong Kong
Tel:(852)95619525

Website:www.billson.cn
E-mail address:cs@billson.cn

First published 2024

Produced by Billson International Ltd
CDPF/01

ISBN 978-1-80377-098-7

© Dulwich College Management Asia Pacific Pte. Ltd. All rights reserved.
The original content within this product remains the property of Dulwich College Management Asia Pacific Pte. Ltd., and cannot be reproduced without prior permission. Updates and derivative works of the original content remain the property of Dulwich College Management Asia Pacific Pte. Ltd. and are provided by Dulwich College Management Asia Pacific Pte. Ltd.
The authors and publisher have made every attempt to ensure that the information contained in this book is complete, accurate and true at the time of printing. You are invited to provide feedback of any errors, omissions and suggestions for improvement.
Every attempt has been made to acknowledge copyright. However, should any infringement have occurred, the publisher invites copyright owners to contact the address below.
Dulwich College Management Asia Pacific Pte. Ltd.
101 Thomson Road, United Square, #19-01/03 Singapore 307591

Dear Reader,

I am delighted to introduce "Voices", the third anthology in our celebrated series showcasing the exceptional literary talents of students across the Education in Motion (EiM) family of schools around the world. This year's collection is truly remarkable as we're exploring new and exciting frontiers.

It's been such a pleasure to visit so many schools, work with so many inspiring teachers and students, and see the beginnings of these concepts form in the students' minds. Getting to read the finished pieces, as you are about to, has been a great experience. A huge well done to those who made it into the collection this year. If you didn't make it in, please know that many entries couldn't be included due to the constraints of curating. Your brilliant and powerful poems were deeply appreciated-thank you for sharing your work with me.

This year's theme, 'Voices,' has been a joy to explore. Thousands of EiM students have delved into the profound significance and privilege of possessing a voice. They've examined what it means to speak up, listen to others, be proud of our unique voices, and the responsibilities we shoulder as individuals with voices in society.

Many poems in this collection reflect this exploration-there are pieces about being loud and proud of who we are, complaints about how we treat our world, and epic ballads meant to be listened to by a crackling fire. You may find yourself listening to the voice of a famous villain or an inanimate object. The variety of approaches to the theme really stood out to me this year.

One of the most thrilling innovations in this year's anthology is the inclusion of QR codes linking to audio recordings of the poets themselves reading their work. This feature adds an extraordinary dimension to the reading experience, offering a magical bridge between the written word and the spoken voice, creating a much deeper connection with the poet and their work. I highly recommend you use your devices to scan these QR codes and see how it changes the experience of reading the poem. For me, it transforms the anthology into a powerful, living time capsule, packed full of life and energy. Additionally, a few of EiM's dedicated teachers have contributed, documenting some of the voices that have provided so much inspiration to their students.

To those whose poems are featured in this anthology, congratulations! Your work is a testament to your courage, insight, and remarkable talent. These poems traverse a spectrum of experiences – from personal triumphs and introspective musings to vibrant character pieces, bold critiques of society, and joyful celebrations of life. Each piece challenges us to think, reflect, and appreciate the power of our own voices.

I wish to extend my deepest gratitude to the extraordinary teachers across the EiM campuses. Your dedication, passion, and unwavering support have been such an inspiration to me throughout this project. It has been a privilege to work with such ambitious, compassionate, and inspiring educators. I am also immensely thankful to Edgar Zillmann (EiM), whose relentless efforts and willingness to take risks made this year's tour and book project possible. Our publishers have been fantastic to work with throughout this series, and we couldn't have made such a high-quality collection without Jenni Harrison and her exceptional copy-editing skills, ensuring each poem shines as brightly as it should.

"Voices" is a celebration of the extraordinary achievements of our young writers. It stands as a testament to their dedication, creativity, and unyielding spirit. As you immerse yourself in their words and listen to their voices, I hope you find as much joy, wisdom, and inspiration as I have.

With heartfelt gratitude,

Mark Grist

CONTENTS

1	**A Boy's Guide** *Sean B*
3	**A Polar Bear's Voice** *Kevin K*
6	**A Spider** *Sabrina W*
7	**A Wish Upon a Birthday Cake** *Caroline L*
9	**An Unforgettable Day** *Melissa T*
11	**Are You Okay?** *Simran P*
13	**Consecrate More Money** *Elena*
14	**Creation Myth** *Claire Z*
16	**Curtain Call** *Caden*
18	**English** *Jacky Y*
19	**From Peter To Wendy** *Amelia P*
20	**Ghosts** *Michelle B*
21	**How To Deal With Failure** *Sejun P*
23	**I Am A Chessboard** *Roger*
24	**I Am A Fire** *Nicole*
25	**I Am A Steak** *Libby*
26	**I'm From a Place Where...** *Elsa Z*
27	**I Heard Your Voice** *Yoyo Y*
28	**Julian** *Julia Z*
29	**King of Koopas** *Maia W*
31	**Looking Away From Ocean Views** *Yashvi K*

33	**Love In Shanghai**	*Alvin W*
34	**Love Poem**	*Nella*
35	**Medusa**	*Serena Q and Serena W*
36	**Microphone**	*Yee*
37	**Mirror, Mirror**	*Yiling Y*
38	**My Brother**	*Grace*
39	**My Brother Muffy**	*Xinning C*
40	**My Cat**	*Nina*
41	**My Dog**	*Del B*
43	**My Turtle**	*Maya E*
44	**My Voice**	*Paula M*
46	**No Longer Voiceless**	*Jimin Y*
48	**Olympus**	*Aadhrith S*
49	**Panic**	*Abi J*
51	**Phone**	*Celine*
52	**Poem**	*Damian T*
53	**Poker Cards**	*Daniel*
55	**Proustian Precipitation – Raindrops of Remembrance**	*Eugenia L*
57	**Scream**	*Ian C*
58	**Shadow**	*Terry L*
59	**Shanghai**	*Yuhang*
60	**Sid**	*Tilda S*
62	**Singularity**	*Wendy*
65	**Snow**	*David W*
66	**Sounds of the World**	*Kingston Z*
68	**Spaceship**	*Brad*
69	**Still, I Try**	*Petra H*
70	**Stress**	*Kyrie C*

71	**Struggling** *Kayley S*
73	**Study** *Leo L*
74	**Sweet Doze** *Sohyi P*
76	**Terminator** *Myles K*
77	**The Among Us Imposter** *Joshua Z and Ocean G*
78	**The Evil Queen** *Cindy W and Una Z*
79	**The Evil Queen's Lament** *Jessie Z*
81	**The Forgotten Soldiers** *Joshua Z*
82	**The Ocean's Embrace** *Callum L*
83	**The One Who Built Ceramic Walls** *Kelly*
85	**The Silent Roar of Us** *Chandana J*
87	**The Sound of Rain** *Karida M*
89	**The Story About Pichon the Knight** *Ian C and Sze W*
91	**The Voice Within** *Jessie Z*
93	**The Voices In My Head** *Michelle B*
95	**The Wolves and the Phantoms** *Ryan Z*
99	**To Me** *Julian*
100	**Untitled** *Ella*
101	**Villains** *Gabriel L, Johnson S and Delon C*
103	**Voice** *Sam W*
104	**Voice** *Shivika*
105	**Voice of Silence** *Chonwai C*
107	**Voice Poem** *Elaine H*
108	**Voice Poem** *Joanna S*
109	**Voices** *Emily K*
110	**Voices** *Aparajita D*
111	**Voices of People** *Taehui L*
112	**Words** *Caroline L*
113	**You Are...** *Alexander Y*

A Boy's Guide

Wear the light chainmail of a smile
Or the heavy armor of the opposite
Don't show the truth,
Don't do the bad thing

Don't show it
Stay strong
Don't look for advice
You are the advice,
Don't do the bad thing

Don't touch
Don't show them yourself
Stay the lone wolf,
Not the one in distress
Not the Cinderella in a dress
Stay the knight in shining armor,
Don't do the bad thing

You don't fear
You don't feel
You are the protector,
Don't do the bad thing

Stay with the pack
Don't wander
Nor stay with it for too long,
Don't do the bad thing
Don't do the bad thing…

You are in chains, in prison, in cuffs.
This is life,
Welcome to being,
A boy.

Sean B
Dulwich College Shanghai Puxi

A Polar Bear's Voice

The ice splinters with a crack around me
And thunders into the gaping mouth
Of a burning sea.

Great iron seals plough through our waters,
Leaving behind a trail of waste
Suffocating all in its wake.

Birds in the air screech,
Howl and scream,
As the sky turns a sickly blue.

It seems like eternity now –

But once there were days,
When we laughed and played in clear blue bays,
Without a care in the world –
The water fine and pure as glass,

And once we felt joy
When we played in the dazzling snow,
Full of zeal and passion
In our Arctic wonderland,

And once we could see the stars –

Looking up in the night sky
How they dazzled with their brilliant glow
Like beacons of hope leading the lost traveler home.

How they shone with a vigor, an intensity
Displaying a universe of endless possibility

The hopes, the dreams, the aspirations
of a generation
Shone in those skies

Now it's all gone.

Our bays tainted black with waste.
The skies darkened into a grey haze,
The air too thick to breathe.
Snow silently receding from view,
The wind hissing and howling in grief.

Smoke billowing out into the skies,
Like dark tendrils of resentment,
Harbored over the years.
Contaminating all with its toxic touch.

The waste flowing into the water,
Tarnishing it forever with its malignant taste.
Our water smeared a permanent shade of black.

And the stars –

The stars are gone,
Faded away into oblivion.

The hopes.
The dreams.
The aspirations.

Of a polar bear,
Who wishes to be heard.

Kevin K
Dulwich College Shanghai Pudong

A Spider

A spider spun its web within my mind,
It bound my thoughts, my voice confined,
Each silken thread a whispered doubt,
Fear's echo, a constant shout.

The mirror mocked, a funhouse hall,
Distorting features, twisting tall.
"Too thin, too fat," the whispers taunt,
Each imperfection and flaws I'd count.

Each ounce of confidence, each itsy bit,
My mind's a lane, memories submit.
Revisiting the past's my ultimate demise,
Nothing else can touch me, I've no kryptonite.

Music is a friend, friends offer a gentle hand,
Siblings offer me solace, still no one understands.
I sing with composure, I dance to the beat,
My hands weave together, I flatten my feet.

They'll whisper flaws, but don't you listen,
Your worth is intrinsic, your heart glistens.
Love yourself deeply, then stand up tall,
Unfurl your wings, let your spirit enthral.

Sabrina W
Dulwich College Seoul

A Wish Upon a Birthday Cake

On my birthday,
I gave my wish to you.

I wished,
for your dreams to stay big,
for you to achieve those dreams,
and then to dream bigger still.
I didn't know that I wouldn't be in those dreams.

I wished,
for your worries to stay small,
for you to live life without the weight of it dragging you down,
for you to be able to find the silver lining, always.
but you thought I was dragging you down.

I wished,
for you to thrive under the burden and pressure of life and not get crushed by it,
for you to never need to carry more than you can hold,
and even when you did, for you to let someone else carry some for you.
I always thought I would be that someone.

I wished,
for your life to become everything you wanted it to,
for you to find your purpose,
your one true passion, and love it forever.
I thought you would love me forever.

But I guess forevers can be cut short.

So now I know.
On my birthday,
I wasted my wish on you.

Caroline L
Dulwich College Shanghai Pudong

An Unforgettable Day

It was a cold night, a time filled with horror,
A night I was wishing that would never come.
I hurried to bed, burying myself away from the terror,
The feeling and thoughts made my body feel numb.

As I lay hopelessly on my bed, I slowly lost consciousness,
My mind became blank, a void of blackness had reached me.
Suddenly I found myself awoken, my mind felt ominous,
I rushed myself and got prepared for what I was going to face.

As time went by, I became more nervous than ever,
My hand was trembling as I walked towards the building.
I walked along with my mother beside me,
We sat beside the room, waiting for my name to be called.

Minutes passed, suddenly a woman came and called my name,
I stood up in fear, slowly walking inside the room.
As I approached the chair, I sat nervously and started playing,
My hands pressed on the keys, touching each and every one.

Seconds turned into minutes, I was still playing.
As I kept going, I started going faster and faster.
My hands were uncontrollable, I couldn't recall anything.
Eventually, I found myself finished with my piece.

A week had passed since the terrifying day had come,
I sat in the dining room, minding my own business.
Suddenly I received a call from a number,
I went over and heard that I passed my exam.

It was a truly unforgettable day.

Melissa T
Dulwich International High School Programme Hengqin

Are You Okay?

Are you okay?
They ask
Is she okay?
They ask
Am I okay?
I ask
I lie
Say yes
Hold my tears
Stop the streams
Let it? But...
Scared
What would they think?
Swallow my emotions and thoughts
The build up of negativity inside my throat
Need to speak and let it go
I do. I let it out
I feel self-determined
I feel a breeze of calm
I feel like I am free from my troubles for a fleeting moment.

Simran P
Dulwich College Seoul

Consecrate More Money

Step into an old mansion with walls in grey.
The wind dashing through your nose, a rancid taste.
Rising heart rate,
the smell of decay.
This ancient place will force you to obey.

How unfortunate it is to step in this state.
Cupboard across the backdoor,
netballs on the lawn,
something really terrifying will appear before dawn.

But does it even matter?
Most of these are fake.
Will it make me scared?
Suppose it's just a piece of cake.
Want to find the history or the truth?
Then you should pay me on YouTube.
Pretend to scream when there's anything "creepy",
my computer apps can create a ghost swinging.
Log in to those accounts, send meaningless emojis,
someone's mind might be stung,
brought down on their knees.
Whatever, please
just consecrate more money.

Elena
Dehong Shanghai International Chinese School

Creation Myth

And God said, Let there be light, and there was light.
Genesis 1:3-25

There was light, coming off the t
to crackle out of God's mouth
like dragon-fire, plowing through
bunnies of intergalactic dust, a gentle-
pronged rake forking paws and ears
to the next galaxy, and the next

until gray substance dissipated
into the hard rock of a waylaid asteroid
and light condensed into a child pressed

against a cupboard door in hide
and seek, ear mouse-folded, eyebrows
whiskering in preparation for a loudening

footstep, bare soles
in mid-air, crouching at some creaking twist
of the handle: *ready, set, go*—evaporating

down Neptune's starred alley, entering
the mouth of the Earth, checkered
blue and green, buttering out: I envision

God was maybe a naked woman
with pink stilettos festooned
around her foot's lemon-branch arch—

that she had a long, spindly tongue
curled around a blue-raspberry
icebreaker like a raccoon's tail

who squinted, and said
                  Let there be light,
her breath dewing Adam's back

as he awakened on the moon
of garden-pebbles,
a dolphin

on the dry shore of history
who unmoored himself and yawned.

Claire Z
Dulwich College Suzhou

Curtain Call

Past the curtain call
the red sheets fall
closing as the heart shrinks.
Bittersweet.

The long walk back home,
darkness, loneliness
tugs at you in the night.
Alone,

recalling, barely
an hour ago.
Adrenaline, washing over you
like a flood.

They clapped, they cheered

your name, among others.
There you all stood, proud
as they called.
Now you call

to nothing but echoes.
The play is done,
recognition was won,
why aren't you happy?

Isolated

you sit there, thinking

months of hard work
led to this, led to you.
Solo under the streetlamps.

Lamps that never shone as bright
as those,
when you were on stage.

Caden
Dulwich College Shanghai Pudong

English

E is for enthusiasm, a creation that brings excitement.
N is for neat, a tidy way to organize your thoughts.
G is for global, the important component in the current world.
L is for lasting, the history of the ancient times.
I is for invention, the tool for innovations.
S is for spirit, an inheritance of the western world's culture.
H is for hope, an entertainment in frustrations.

English, a language worth learning.

Jacky Y
Dulwich International High School Programme Hengqin

From Peter To Wendy

In the heart of Neverland I long to stay,
Where hopes can soar and worries float away.
I'll fly above, unbound and free,
In eternal youth, how I wish I could be.

To linger in childhood's inviting hold
Where innocence reigns, a soul of pure gold.
But as time tiptoes forward, it begins to make way
For an everlasting shadow, drawing closer by day.

Reluctant steps I take, dejected, my eyes cast down.
Afraid of wearing the weight of reality's crown.
Yet amidst the somber, gloomy and grim,
A light guides me, the path no longer dim.

Through endless skies, the North Star glows,
Beams casting away the dark of my anxious woes.
For growing up isn't forgetting all we hold dear,
But finding new wonders, without any fear.

Amelia P
Dulwich College Seoul

Ghosts

We are ghosts.
We are the superiors
All the other baddies are our inferiors
We float through the walls
Haunting
Taunting
Swords come flying through our bodies
As we pass through the armies
Everyone knows us
Everyone fears us
We are the best.
We will always be rejoiced
We will always be the cursed
And we will always leave you in the dirt.

Michelle B
Dulwich College Shanghai Puxi

How To Deal With Failure

Did you all have that one time,
When you got called a failure?
Happens to me, honestly,
While I think of me as a crystal,
The others think I'm a pistol,
Inferior to a rifle
Or I think of me, as a cup half full,
While the others tell me I'm a cup half empty,
Telling me I'm dull, drastic, a degenerate,
Almost gives me that bittersweet emotion
While I'm happy, others think there's better
And I try to think: ya know what, let her,
Go beat them and say: it's my pleasure,
I'm immune to your pester,
Because when you believe them, not you,
They'll swerve you to the ground,
While others get ahead, you'll be stuck in a pool
And even if you fail, play it back,
It's not anything anyone's going to condemn,
Stand back up – try it again,
Do it one more time – you might get it then.

Sejun P
Dulwich College Seoul

I Am A Chessboard

I am a chessboard.
I hear the weapons crashing together.
I see black and white are having a war,
Many piece like the knight, queen, king, pawn, rook, and bishop, are fighting on me.
They are heavy like mountains and that feeling is not a joke.
But when it is over, I can taste many kinds of victory and loss.
I think about victory always, but it has loss and ties.
I like to taste good like victory, but I cannot.
I am afraid of loss every way.
I dream of always victory and no more loss or ties.

Roger
Dehong Shanghai International Chinese School

I Am A Fire

I am a fire.
I see some people running away from me.
I can hear the people scream, and the people crying.
I hugged the trees and I hugged the house, and they broke.
One time I was eating oil, and it was so yummy.
I think about why many people wanted to get away from me.
I love to give people warmth.
I'm afraid of the people putting water on my body.
I dream of being people's good friend, and they play with me.

Nicole
Dehong Shanghai International Chinese School

I Am A Steak

I am a steak...
I can see the fire under me,
And the saliva groping out from
Children's mouth.
I hear people's tummy growling, and
I can feel the pan under me getting
hotter and hotter.
I'm very yummy!
I wonder what it will look like in people's
Tummies, if it will be fun.
And I love to swim in the soy sauce!
I'm really afraid that if the children don't
Like to eat me, then I will go in the trash!
I wish I could fly, then I could sleep on
The tree, and no one could find me.

Libby
Dehong Shanghai International Chinese School

I'm From a Place Where...

I'm from a place where buildings are high,
Always reaching for the sky,
They never stop growing.

I'm from a place where traffic jams happen,
And people go crazy.
Where prices are high,
Everything is expensive,
Nothing is cheap.
You may become fatter,
But your wallet will be thinner.

Where people love mumbling,
Where cafés start bubbling.
Where birds begin chirping,
Where the sun's always rising.

I'm from a place called Shanghai.

Elsa Z
Dehong Shanghai International Chinese School

I Heard Your Voice

I heard your voice,
It was the footsteps of spring.
I heard your voice,
It was the sound of plants beginning to grow.
I heard your voice,
It was the willow swaying like it was brushing her head.
I heard your voice,
It was the birds singing in the branches.
I heard your voice,
It was the sound of snow melting.
I heard your voice,
It was the sound of the river taking off its coat of ice.

Yoyo Y
Dulwich International High School Programme Hengqin

Julian
(Inspired by 'Wonder' by R. J. Palacio)

I'm Julian,
August is the worst,
With his ugly face, it looks like it could burst,
I have never seen such an ugly face before,
To look at him, I can't do it anymore,
I am not like that kid, I have a lot of followers,
All he'd be good for, is being a sword swallower,
The guys always follow me,
Miles, Henry, Amos,
They know who their leader is,
They know I'm the boss,
Even Jack Will became my follower,
Poor August doesn't have a partner,
I am the role model at the school,
All the teachers like me,
My parents are the school's sponsors,
That's why in school I am a super star,
I deserved everything I have at school,
Which August can never have.

Julia Z
Dulwich College Shanghai Puxi

King of Koopas

With a set of yellowed fangs, and a pair of sharp claws,
I rise into the night you've got to give me applause.
I am Bowser – the King of the Koopas,
The one that's handsome – totally not random.
I'm not a dinosaur,
But certainly, more valuable than a diamond ore.
Surely with these looks, these astounding spikes,
Princess Peach will finally find someone that she likes.
Which is not that stubby, little mushroom eater.
For Mario is his name, his hair could certainly be neater.
His horrendous moustache is extremely immature,
Luckily, he isn't a successful entrepreneur
Like me. My business, clearly close to capturing him and his brother.
But the profit I'm looking for is not even Peach.
What I devour, what I crave, I will never teach.
Power. That's what. Me, the ruler!
Only I can steal the Super Star from the Penguin King.
Only I can create the power that can reach all the way to Beijing.
Only I am selfish – a true, stinky leader.
Only I can turn a Koopa into a bleeder.
I may cause a lot of drama,
But hey! I'm the King of Lava.
With my castle, surrounded by darkness,
It's my kingdom, full of evil and harshness.
You may think other villains are better –
But you're wrong, I'm the best, always and forever.
The Joker, stopped every time by the black-masked dude.

Miss Trunchbull, scared away by a five-year-old girl – how crude!
But I have never been defeated.
And wait – there's more: I'm better than those who retreated:
I can play the piano.
I bet none of you can do it! You'll never beat me!
You'll never beat the Koopa King – don't you dare disagree!

Maia W
Dulwich College Shanghai Puxi

Looking Away From Ocean Views

My future is a painting.
A painting of the ocean.
I paddle endlessly in my wooden boat,
Barely afloat with my battered sails,
Just to capture that perfect view.

The further I row,
The more lost I become...
Lost at sea
In a pool of my judgment.

I sit here, daily,
In my palm, a clean canvas.
As I try to capture the sun setting on the waters,
My fingers work magic with my acrylic paints.

But I erase every brush stroke.
I rethink every decision.
And as the sunset wafts away from me,
My canvas lies bare, cream white once again.

As I sit here every day,
With no change. No progress.
I never quite realize that–

My future, it's a painting.
A painting of the ocean.
And I'm so caught up in its brush strokes,
I'm not enjoying today's sunset view.

Yashvi K
Dulwich College Shanghai Pudong

Love In Shanghai

Love in Shanghai;
Excitement always high!
With my love as we drive,
Looking up towards the sky,
Clouds covering our eyes,
Suddenly time turns to night;
Street music shines bright,
Impressions carved upon my mind,
Motivating my impulses
To take food that is nice,
Pork mixed with fried egg rice.
Such yummy food!
It even makes me cry.
But the car alarm takes me
Back to my mind
Belly slowly inflates
And rises.

I close my eyes, rest my mind,
Silently enjoy the beauty
With my love at my side.
Together we watch
This spectacular Shanghai
Celebrations in our minds never end.
Love in Shanghai.

Alvin W
Dehong Shanghai International Chinese School

Love Poem

I wake up and you are all I think of
I go to bed and you are all I dream of
There's no way to escape the thought of you
There's no way to forget your presence, your existence
You brought me sunshine, when I only saw rain
You brought me joy when I only felt pain
I'm sorry for lying and not telling you how I feel
But what's the point if I know how this story will end?
The way you will look at me next
The feeling of disgust
The look in your eyes
I couldn't bear getting hurt that much
By the boy that I most trust.

Nella
Dulwich College Shanghai Pudong

Medusa

Greetings, mortals, I'm Medusa,
I can turn people into stone.
I dwell in my cave in silence,
But no one can stop me when I sit upon my throne.
When Perseus slew me out of spite,
I sank deep into Tartarus.
I bid my time planning revenge,
For us sisters, as I'm one of us.
One day I will avenge my former life,
Before I throw it away.
Once I rise out of the pit,
I'll make the world sway.
The lord of seas once had me in his dreams,
But I'm tired of his little games,
Lies, manipulation, it's all the same,
For he left me to Athena's schemes.
What do you think I am? A meme?!
Anyway, this is just a waste of my time
As I will rise once more.
To lead an endless rule of evil,
To give myself and my sisters a treat,
As I feast upon your rotten meat!

Serena Q and Serena W
Dulwich College Shanghai Puxi

Microphone

I am a microphone,
So small and black,
I touch human hands, all humans,
And listen to singers repeating their songs.
It's so fun to sing along,
Then I taste the dust which is sweet like candy.
In the night, birds fly by, chirping so sweetly,
Leaves floating saying, "Hello!"
I have a fear of water and fire.
I wish I could write my own song and sing it out loud.

Yee
Dehong Shanghai International Chinese School

Mirror, Mirror

Mirror, mirror on the wall,
Am I the fairest of them all?
The brightest, most endearing in your view?
Speak truth, mirror, don't obscure what's true.

"Yes, my lady," the mirror replies,
Yet within its glass, a hollow guise.

"He loves me, he loves me not," I murmur,
Hope flickering, fervent dreams to confer.
"He loves me, he loves me not," I plea,
But each petal's a verdict, a cruel decree.

For as the final petal wanes from view,
Clouded delusions drift, unveiling skies of blue.

The day arrives, turmoil brews within,
Yet I muster courage to confront my sin.
"Do you love yourself?" I ask, with fear.
Amid the water's reflection, a monster appears.

"No," I answer, shedding my disguise,
And with one final breath, devoid of lies
I plunge into the basin of my demise.

Yiling Y
Dulwich College Seoul

My Brother

To me, you are a sour blueberry,
You are a bouncing fire that won't stay still,
You are a fresh lotus ready to blossom,
And a noisy band that isn't in sync,
You are a sleepy read of an exciting book,
And a journey to every site in the world,
You are a shiny crystal in a dull cave,
You are my comfort when I'm afraid,
To me you are my universe,
Even though we bicker and fight,
You are my brother.

When we are older, all I can hope,
Is that we will forever be together,
I hope that with whatever comes,
We will not lose sight of the most important thing,
Wherever you are,
You will be in my heart,
I know we will fight,
I cannot deny it,
But I love you so much,
I will always be your big sister.

Grace
Dulwich College Shanghai Pudong

My Brother Muffy

I have a little brother called Muffy.
Although he is small, he is a real toughie.
He is so smart and funny,
His favorite toy is his white bunny.
He likes to laugh and play,
And he happily does this all day.
I love my little brother, he is cute.
I only wish that sometimes he would mute.

Xinning C
Dulwich College Suzhou

My Cat

I have a cat,
who is really weird,
he stares when he's sat,
and he has a beard.

He doesn't walk like others,
he twirls in the air,
that scares his brothers,
I think he's quite rare.

He knows all languages,
people say he's so nice,
he knows how to tie bandages,
he never tortures mice.

I love my weird cat,
who is pretty fat,
he is best of all kittens,
and he wears mittens.

Nina
Dehong Shanghai International Chinese School

My Dog

My dog Satimo is so slow,
Especially when jumping in the snow.
His favorite food is his bone,
And he loves to nibble on Daddy's phone.
In his bed he likes to sleep,
All his treasures he likes to keep.
He is my love and joy,
Although he broke my newest toy.

Del B
Dulwich College Suzhou

My Turtle

My turtle hates being fed,
He also hates getting out of bed.
He just sits around in his tank,
And dreams about robbing a bank.
He is small and green,
And a little bit mean.
He is special to me,
I like to let him be.

Maya E
Dulwich College Suzhou

My Voice

I have a voice.
To speak to my mind
To express my pain
Explain my cries.

I have a voice.
To say right or wrong
To sing song
To reach out to those I need.

I have a voice.
To advocate for causes
To pray without ceasing
To stand for my self.

I have a voice.
To express my feelings
To speak out for my self
To heal from within.

I have a voice.
To be me
To dream
To love.

I have a voice.
To write
To accomplish and

Appreciate all the things
I have done.

Paula M
Dulwich College Seoul

No Longer Voiceless

How would it feel being truly voiceless?
No matter how much you try
you will always be choiceless,
with no way to shout nor cry.

When an attempt is made to yell,
you are soon blocked and blamed
from getting out of their dark-hushed cell.
You are forced to stand inside, in shame.

The only thing you can do is silently wait
until you're brave enough to share your voice again.
But all those struggles are just tempting bait
for the monsters who come with anger and chains.

They say you are a fool with no opinions,
but they are filled with lies and false hopes.
Jealous, they come spouting billions
of jabs and jibes. You feel tangled in their ropes.

Forever speechless and naïve.
nobody can listen to your long rants
of dreams and aspirations you can't achieve,
but your voice will grow just like a plant.

You will arise bigger, and the monsters will run
from the power of your voice. It starts in a timid hum,
but it grows and grows till all sides split.
And the real you climbs back out of their pit.

Their ropes become your ladder, their chains
become your weapon. They look for new pain
but now you menace them, and they know... never again.

Jimin Y
Dulwich College Seoul

Olympus

Zeus, the king, he ruled the sky,
Poseidon was the sea,
Hades, the last brother, he was death.
Hera, she was queen,
Demeter, the sister, she was crops,
The eldest sister Hestia, she was fire.
Ares, son of Zeus, he was bloody war,
Athena, she was tactics,
Dionysus, he was wine,
Hermes, he was thievery.
Artemis was the moon,
Her brother, Apollo, was the sun,
And finally, Aphrodite. She was love and beauty.

Aadhrith S
Dulwich College Seoul

Panic

In a world of fleeting thoughts, a dance of the mind
Feelings and the move of the tongue unwinds
With opinions and words that bundle like leaves
Figure of speech likes to run away, fleet

A kaleidoscope of colors and images collide.
Like an arrow that likes to bend me and bind
I dance in confusion and flail in air
My brain starts to burst bubble and tear

To step out of frame is to step out of line
And to cry is to scream out to others it's fine
And to call out for help is to overreact
And to not feel bad is a trait that I lack

But to overreact is a to show how I feel
Because I crave something that others can't heal
'Cause I long to unhinge and I long to be free
But that's just a dream, there's something wrong about me

Emotions command, the brain demands
It seems all so clear, but blurred like a dance
Fingers pick and peck and my tongue falls so loose
My body is numb now like bruises, black, blue

Muscle claustrophobic under my skin
I tear away to let out what's within
Tears race down like a curtain of rain
I scratch away and steal regardless of the pain

People tilt their heads worried about what's wrong
As I find myself lost and dumbfounded mid-song
Like claws at a carcass my nails engrave
Till the back of my hand is torn and concave

Red runs wild like jaguars in heat
Droplets clutch on to my skin like feet
They sting like spiders, black widows that bite
Flesh breaks free like the moon breaks through the night.

But once they leave, when footsteps fade out.
My tears are now dry like dirt in a drought.
My heart slows its beat, and my shoulders untwine.
And I sit in my peace, my longevity.

Abi J
Dulwich College Shanghai Pudong

Phone

I am a phone, a boring old phone,
Spending days cramped in a hand.
All my days are spent watching an ancient face picking his nose,
All my life, hearing voices loud and brutal,
Spoken in a foreign language.
Sometimes I can eat sweet batteries on the weekends,
And take a breath from the hard jabs of fingers at the end,
But, I still yearn for the days of peace,
Of days when only gentle voices sing,
Of weeks of sweet batteries and sleeping,
Oh how I shall yearn.

Celine
Dehong Shanghai International Chinese School

Poem

Writing poems about voices is too much effort,
I'd rather fall face first into some dirt,
But if I do not write a poem about voices,
I will fail and appear dumb,
So I am writing this unwillingly.
Oh, this is stupidity.

I don't want to do this anymore,
But then my English teacher will start a war
With me, and I will be
The laughing stock of my family tree.
But who really cares?
It's not like they're going to banish me downstairs,
So, I will stop writing this.

Damian T
Dulwich College Seoul

Poker Cards

I am a set of poker cards,
I taste tobacco smoke
And hear people giving bets.
"I bet a dollar that I get a six in 26 throws!"
I feel hands grasp me
And see dice lying on tables.

I think about my dreams,
Hoping they come true,
And all those dreams
Are about games.
I hope that one day,
I'll get to be the king of cards,
And win every game.
After all, I am a set of poker cards.

Daniel
Dehong Shanghai International Chinese School

Proustian Precipitation – Raindrops of Remembrance

In the misty cold air, leaves cascade from skeletal trees,
Howling wind wails, rain pitter-patters from the charcoal clouds.
Lightning flickers through barren branches,
Birds flee, carrying their chronicles to the distant lands.

Gazing up, but the clouds elude my searching eyes.
Bowing my head down, but teardrops tumble on the Earth.
Raindrops slither on my window,
Reflecting tears streaming down my face.

Ripples arise from the falling leaves on the clear, deep, burgundy pond.
In its depths, forgotten memories awake,
My nerves alight with quivers,
As if a ghost in my heart begins to resurrect.

Stirring up echoes of childhood's forsaken tales,
Locking up whispers of yesteryear in concealed clouds.
Raindrops tell their stories from the water cycle,
And the past, relentlessly, emerges from tears.

Pictures and pictures of faded footprints escape from memory's vault,
My heart then breaks from the evocative wind.
The enshrined memories bring me back to the past euphoria,
Where melancholy does not exist.

With voices hushed, their cherished names echo in my mind,
Fables turned into imprints, like time's tapestry.
Recalling caresses and bedtime stories, their caring spirit imbues.
Amidst shared moments, their gentle embrace warms my heart.

Grandparents' wisdom, a beacon light,
Guiding me through my life, shining so bright.
Though they live beyond heaven's veil,
Their love and kindness still pave a trail.

As nature stops weeping tears,
The pizzicato of memorabilia in my soul ceases in sears.
I honour their spirits, forever free.
In this sublime memory, their essence lives on, an eternal symphony.

Eugenia L
Dulwich International High School Programme Hengqin

Scream

I could scream and scream, calling for help,
my desperate pleas never noticed,
like a wild animal, my claims fought,
all vanished with the wave of a hand.
My soul degraded, distraught, shattered
into pieces. When you pick them back up,
you glue them together, and I can't interrupt,
rejected and denied all over again.
My desperate pleas, bottling them up,
hiding the growing monster inside me,
clawing at my heart from the inside out,
choking my trap shut, drowning in silence.
Nothing to it, I could scream for hours.
I would scream for hours upon hours.

Ian C
Dulwich College Seoul

Shadow

When I am alone, my voice is a whispering shadow
When I am enraged, my voice is a roaring storm
It is a blood-curdling scream when I confront my fears
And when I tread through haunted halls and corridors,
Whispers surround me, like ghostly troubadours.
One day my voice will be a haunting melody,
A macabre symphony, invoking dread and glee.
And I will use it to break all the peace and love.

Terry L
Dulwich International High School Programme Hengqin

Shanghai

I'm from a place where everything is famous,
Where there's a Disney and you could see fireworks.
There are the three skyscrapers of Lujiazui,
All gazing across the Huangpu River at the old buildings on Shanghai Bay.

I'm from a place that's full of technology,
Where everybody is socializing but only digitally.
Wherever you go, either in malls, buses or metros,
You see people enjoying their phone, laptop, or Nintendo.

I'm from a place where hopes are high,
A city where people expect opportunities called Shanghai.
Young elites step into this city,
Immersed in the air as if smelling for money.

I'm from a place that's tiring to be,
Libraries full of exhausted students, forbidden from watching TV.
You hear every day the laughter coming out from mansions,
But also, the sighs of the delivery men – wondering why they have so much pressure.

Shanghai is a gorgeous place for many that came,
But also, a city where nothing is a game.
Everything you see that makes you astonished,
Comes from the workers that strive to make it polished.

Yuhang
Dulwich College Shanghai Pudong

Sid

I am Sid,
The most menacing boy in town.
I bring terror upon my bedroom toys,
Where it's all about to go down.

Crack them, punch them, chop them, rip them, pull them down the stairs,
Stab them, kick them, throw them, dunk them, who even cares?
Tie them to a rocket and light it on fire,
Or chuck them on a street where they get run over by a tire!

I'm a menacing little boy, anything to destroy a toy.
I rip off their heads, to make horrible new ones,
Like spiders with baby doll heads, or Barbies with multiple arms.

I rule this neighborhood, that's just what bullies do,
They don't dare to look me in the eye and see my horrible face.
And I despise school if you were wondering,
Because I just HATE that place!

The one thing I am scared of,
The one thing that I fear.
Is that sometimes they walk, sometimes they talk,
My creations come alive.

They prank me,
They hurt me.

They make me scream in pain!

But that will NEVER stop me,
For I will rise AGAIN!

Tilda S
Dulwich College Shanghai Puxi

Singularity

Lover, can you hear me scream?
Whisper these sweet nothings into a swirling
Dark maelstrom of miniscule infinities.
There is no sound in space but perhaps if
I yell loud enough something will keep
Spinning, spinning, hurtling
And hit you, like rain hits a windshield before the cyclone
Picks you up and swallows you whole.

Each morning I pray I might
Regurgitate you, on the count of
Three, merge shoulder blades with
Stardust so you can feel daylight,
Boiling, racing, seething through your veins
And see what shadowless darkroom I've snared you in.

Lover, I am the singularity of a starless supernova that
Whispers at night, "I'm hungry, I'm hungry, I starve, feed me more,"
but I swallow and I always stay empty.

I remain when the universe blows its fuse
And extinguishes all its altar candles, closes every eye, just
To sink into the ground and rot.
But it is cold like frosted bone, so sharp that
My fingers go blue and stiff and numb and
Yet I still offer to be your kindling
So you can warm yourself with
The embers of my fading ashes.

Lover, I am scared
For all things take their last breath with a conscience that
Knows they are loved and if not, at least
Remembered by all those flickering lights in their midnight canvas and
Slate grey stones that frame their bed.
But when I am full and done and reach the end and I decide to rest,
Lover, who will bury me?

Wendy
Dulwich College Shanghai Pudong

Snow

Snowing in the shadow.
Silent snowflakes dance with grace.
A silent dark, a silver spark,
Blankets the world in a winter dark.

Moonlight whispers on the frozen ground,
A pure silence, without a sound.
Nature's nocturnal,ice looks like art,
Snowflakes weave dreams in the still, black heart.

David W
Dulwich International High School Programme Hengqin

Sounds of the World

In mountains and by the sea, in every corner of the world,
Different sounds interweave, creating a symphony of the earth.
The operatic tones of Chinese opera, like the flowing stream,
The jazz of America, as soft as a breeze passing by,
The singing of India, as the sound of the Ganges River,
The rhythms of Africa, as the heartbeat of the Earth.

The howling of the wind echoes in the valleys,
The gentle caress of rain whispers in the leaves.
Each leaf, each grain of sand,
Tells its own story.

Listen, the Japanese bell,
Clear and melodious, like a cherry blossom falling on the surface of the water,
The Aboriginal drumbeat of Australia,
Deep and passionate, like the waves crashing against the shore.
The Indian mantras,
Eternal and serene, like the flowing river of the Ganges.
The French church bell,
Delicate and melodic, like the wind passing by the Seine.

This is the Symphony of Sounds, the diverse sounds of the world,
They weave together, creating a symphony of the Earth.
Wherever we are,
Whatever language we speak,
We can hear,

The diverse sounds of the world.

Let us cherish this Symphony of Sounds,
Let us listen with our hearts,
Feel, understand,
The diverse sounds of the world.

Kingston Z
Dulwich International High School Programme Hengqin

Spaceship

I am a spaceship,
I hear my bottom rumbling, an asteroid crashing,
I can see the Earth dimming, another planet approaching,
Gobbling for Martian soil, or maybe even rocks or dust,
As I gasp for air in the sandstorm,
I have a fear of alien bombardments, no matter if they even exist,
When am I going back to Earth, I wonder,
As I dream of how I was blasted into space,
As a spaceship, I just want to go back to Earth.

Brad
Dehong Shanghai International Chinese School

Still, I Try

My chest is bright, my heart is filled,
my brain is vast with things I like.
My soul is kind. Still, I try.
My eyes, they fear and yet they love,
I sit, and I breathe the things I feel guilty of.

I like you, you, and you.
I want them to know,
I want them to see,
and yet, my fear is all I will ever be.

My legs are stiff,
my heart is racing,
my mind tells me that's enough waiting.
My throat stumbles with fear as I make a friendly gesture.
But their judging eyes, their silent smirks.
It's all a delusion in my head; they never wanted to be my friend.
So, I stop and think, maybe it's better if I don't try at all.

Drops of grief pour down,
but a little light still shines.
They may smile when they see me frown,
but I'm not trying to change their minds.
I'm trying to find friends who value what they see.
So, I try. I try not for them; I try for me.
Still, it's hard, still, it hurts.
But still, they will see the value of the real me.

Petra H
Dulwich College Seoul

Stress

Mountain on my shoulders
Makes me feel shorter
I take out a key from my folder
Made by silver but more like a killer
The consolation that can take me to heaven
Give me a hand to make me feel less pain in this terrestrial prison
I always request the thing I can not achieve
I do not want to talk about this, may I leave?

Kyrie C
Dulwich International High School Programme Hengqin

Struggling

I can still hear your screams and I wonder
would you ever forgive me?
Would you now be disappointed in my choices?
Because I would be.
I wish somebody would wipe my memories,
Then I could live free.
Without remembering the battles not considered victories.
The path I chose won't ever take me where I want to go,
These voices in my head, they grow and they grow.
The sound of your laughter rings in my ears,
Everything I could have had, left behind.
I'm sorry I didn't know our days left together were timed.
Do you think I would have ever found out on my own
How it's my fault I'm all alone?
Do you look for me to see if I'm suffering?
Watch me now just to see me struggling.

Kayley S
Dulwich College Seoul

Study

Studying hard, morning to night,
Obtain knowledge, shining bright.
Books and notes, my faithful guide,
In their wisdom, I confide.

Challenges come, but I won't fear,
For with hard work, success is near.
Every lesson, every test,
Prepares me for what comes next.

Leo L
Dulwich International High School Programme Hengqin

Sweet Doze

I like to sleep
For hours and hours
Submerged in the deep
Placid pleasure of leisure

I could sleep for an eternity
If only I was not disturbed by my unfinished tasks
That I've left haunting me with tenacity
I cannot escape to relief

My eyelids become more and more heavy
They can't resist sliding down
Then my head starts to lose sanity
I am drifting away from my consciousness

But still I cannot leave myself to waft away
Though I know the weary aftermath
Of massive fatigue will pursue me the next day
I force my worn-out pieces to stay awake

It is my own karma and fate that I've chosen
And a result of failing to control myself but
The pain and agony was an overdose
Torturing me from performing any kind of function

Having to experience
Endless headaches and
Lacking cognitive function is
Painful, just painful

I regret so much that I didn't sleep
I love to sleep
I just want to sleep

Sohyi P
Dulwich International High School Programme Hengqin

Terminator

Puny humans, I'm the Terminator,
The biggest eradicator,
A cyborg-like alligator,
The scariest man there will ever be,
No one better to be seen,
Bowser's got no chance,
He can't even figure out romance,
Peach is just sat there waiting,
While I have a perfect stance,
Every single person in sight,
I'll always put up a fight,
Firing my machine gun,
BANG!!! Down they go,
Blood leaks then they are gone,
Joker, Joker, I'll put you in the toaster,
Butter it up and then I'm gonna eat ya,
Voldemort I hear they call you 007,
0 hair,
0 nose,
And 7 horcruxes,
You're busted
Then it comes to the end,
The bragging is done,
I've had all my fun,
I'd just like to say,
I'll be back.

Myles K
Dulwich College Shanghai Puxi

The Among Us Imposter

I'm the only impostor.
I am the worst disaster.
I am the best abuser.
I always win the poker that involves a lot of murder.
They whisper.
I massacre.
Oh, how I love manslaughter.
It will be with me forever.
I am the best assaulter, the best blackmailer,
and the best gladiator.
After all, I am the imposter,
I might turn into you...

Joshua Z and Ocean G
Dulwich College Shanghai Puxi

The Evil Queen

I am an evil queen,
Who always wants to be eighteen.
Do not make a sound except a whisper,
I'm the most beautiful, you stupid mirror.
Mirror saw my beauty,
I let you eat an apple that's fruity.
Let's make a deal,
Do not dare to steal
I let you to drink the potion,
But drink with your imagination.
Everyone thinks I'm evil,
But I think we need to be equal.
Is she a queen?
Of course she's not.
I'm the queen of them all,
So, bend your knees and crawl.

Cindy W and Una Z
Dulwich College Shanghai Puxi

The Evil Queen's Lament

In the depths of my dark domain,
I reign, a queen of wicked fame,
They tremble at my icy stare,
For I'm the mistress of despair.

I gaze into my mirror's cold embrace,
And see the face of beauty, a wicked grace,
My skin, as smooth as moonlit snow,
A reflection of my inner glow.

Mirror, mirror on the wall,
Who's the fairest of them all?
It must be me; I demand it to be,
No one can match my beauty, you'll see.

Disguised in beauty, veiled in lies,
I drink the poison of my own device,
In the castle that I call my own,
I weave my schemes upon my throne.

They wonder why I'm so unkind,
But they're blind to the turmoil in my mind,
The mirror reflects the truth they shun,
A heart that's fractured, a soul undone.

My small, brown eyes, they tell no lies,
My long, pointy nose, a symbol of my guise,
They see a villain, a fearsome sight,
But inside, I'm lost in endless night.

Through red petal lips, I whisper and moan,
Aching for a love I've never known,
They call me evil, a queen of dread,
But they don't see the tears I've shed
With my beauty so original,
Why am I still written into the list of criminals?

So here I sit, upon my throne,
A queen of darkness, on my own,
Longing for a different fate,
But trapped within my own cruel state.

I demand my voice to be heard.

Jessie Z
Dulwich College Shanghai Puxi

The Forgotten Soldiers

All seems peaceful,
Suddenly sirens start wailing,
Screaming as if they are in despair.
The bombs raining mercilessly.
Rushing out their doors,
Mothers and their children in tow.
Ratata! Ratata! Ratata! go the guns.
Chaos raining, guns raging.
BOOM! CRASH! BOOM!

As soldiers rush out their barracks,
Once kids,
Now bearing the heavy weight of their countries.
Their little hands once filled with toys,
Now attempting to load the weapons poised to destroy.
Their innocent look, now replaced with a ghost of their past,
Bullets tearing through flesh,
An endless stream of blood.
Yet they plow on, though they know death is coming,
A testament to their determination.

CRACK!
Goes the gun of the enemy,
And another child in war falls with grace,
And they depart this world without a trace.
Let this be a reminder,
Of how wars destroy.
Once innocent schoolboys,
Now lie dead in a graveyard.

Joshua Z
Dulwich College Shanghai Puxi

The Ocean's Embrace

I've always felt a deep connection to the ocean,
A world teaming with life both grand and small.
Its vastness and serenity, they captivate my soul,
A place where dreams are born, and stories are told.

As the tide ebbs and flows, my spirit dances too,
In harmony with the rhythm, a symphony of blue.
The ocean's whispers, they sing a melody to me,
A siren's call that beckons endlessly.

With each gentle wave, a treasure unfurls,
A world beneath the surface, a realm of swirling whorls.
Its mysteries unravel, as I delve deeper in,
A testament to the power and grace within

The sound of waves, a soothing song
As I walk the shore where I belong
In the ocean's embrace, I am whole.
Connected to its depths, by heart and soul.

Callum L
Dulwich International High School Programme Hengqin

The One Who Built Ceramic Walls

Group projects.

Usually, I would've really liked those sessions
Pouring out my quirky thoughts without any concession
Develop into resolutions no one would anticipate
And come to a conclusion that would be the best to rate, but:

Wait.

Is anybody listening?
Your eyes are staring far away
I don't know where you're focusing.
Voices echoing, my voice is fading, vanishing
Becoming disassembled words like Jenga blocks collapsing

Is anybody listening?
I see you in the distance gathered somewhere in the lighting:
A distance that would only take a dozen steps to cover;
A distance that would seem to take forever so I hover

So I wait, I'm by myself.

I'm hoping you would turn around
I'm hoping you would care
I'm hoping you don't let me down
I'm hoping you're aware
That I'm feeling isolated in a castle of my own;

Please don't leave me stranded,
I hate being alone.

And if you wonder:

Who built these castle walls?
Who would lock themself up in some wall ten meters tall?

Listen.

They're not meant to be a barrier
I'm sorry if you realize you need a small endeavor

However

You will figure once you try:
It only takes a word of warmth
And soon, the walls will die;

Please, I'm telling you it's getting late
Dusk will soon arrive, and I will still await
The breeze is killing me, an invisible knife
It cuts me down so deeply, in the cold of the night
So—

Please rescue me alive.
Don't leave me here to strive.
I'm struggling to survive.

Kelly
Dulwich College Shanghai Pudong

The Silent Roar of Us

This world we are in,
The world we grow up in, is definitely not a perfect place.
The times we are in,
The struggles we go through,
Make us feel that we advance at a different pace.
The struggles of us women,
Make us feel that we lag behind.
"Women can't vote," said men of old,
Unknowing that those words have started a war.
Balding and enjoying their lavish luxuries made of gold,
Drinking and drinking till they drown in their sorrows,
While being cleaned up after the women, who would soon be their bane.
And thus, the uprising began, the Suffragettes, Rosa Parks, Emmeline Pankhurst,
All strong women, making sure the world hung onto every note.
Susan B. Anthony, Frida Kahlo, and Malala Yousufzai, in them we kept our hope.
All the work of these women,
Let girls like me know that what the future holds is good.
Rosa Parks, Sylvia Rivera, Chimamanda Ngozi Adichie,
These powerful women, never made us waver,
Stood with their heads tall,
With burdens of society and pressures of all,
Let girls like me know that what the future holds is good.
The trust in the world, that's given to women, makes me wonder,

Why are we still not considered the best of them all?

Chandana J
Dulwich College Shanghai Pudong

The Sound of Rain

The sound of rain, a soft song,
A symphony of raindrops, soft and sweet,
Falling from the sky with a beat.
Every raindrop tells a story,
It also talks about growth.
A clean shower, pure and real.
There was a sound on the roof,
The melody of nature.
Despite the pain, life goes on,
In the smooth, healing sound of rain.
So let it wash away your fear,
Wash away the tears.
Because in the soft singing of the rain,
You will find the strength to carry on.

Karida M
Dulwich International High School Programme Hengqin

The Story About Pichon the Knight

I'm not the best at making up stories,
but still sit back and enjoy and don't call it boring.
Once upon a time there was a big bad dragon,
it was born in the middle of a conestoga wagon.
The dragon destroyed everything in sight,
whatever it sees it must take a bite.
As the dragon got older it got stronger and stronger,
and as it grew stronger its skin became tougher.
And soon it surely became a horror,
and of course it caused a reign of terror.
One day a brave, valiant knight,
decided it was time to make things right.
The knight named Pichon headed towards the kitchen,
he equipped himself with utensils in good condition.
The knight headed out of the castle full of hope,
after waving goodbye to the pope
he walked over mountains, hills, and a lake,
"Where is the dragon for goodness' sake?"
Finally he saw the dragon and shouted, "Behold!"
Oh but did I mention the knight's only six years old?
The little knight charged at the dragon with all his might,
about to pounce and about to fight.
The knight started attacking with his spoon and knife,
risking his short little life.
And if you think this is going to be a classical story,
where the good beats evil but that's so boring.
So the dragon looked down at the tiny little child,
and on his face appeared a smile.

It opened his mouth and lowered his head,
and ate him up like he was bread.

And that's the story of Pichon the knight,
so kids, don't fight dragons, go fly your kites.

Ian G, Constantin P and Sze W
Dulwich College Shanghai Pudong

The Voice Within

In the stillness of the night, a whisper breaks,
A symphony of words unspoken,
The voice within, a soul awakes,
In every heart, a promise token.

It is the voice that speaks to us in moments of doubt,
The voice that guides us through the darkness,
The voice that reminds us of our worth,
And the voice that inspires us to greatness.

It is the voice that tells us to keep going,
When the road ahead seems long and hard,
The voice that urges us to take a chance,
And the voice that helps us find our way.

It is the voice that speaks to us in our dreams,
The voice that tells us to follow our hearts,
The voice that reminds us of our passions,
And the voice that helps us find our purpose.

It is the voice that speaks to us in our darkest moments,
The voice that tells us to be strong,
The voice that reminds us of our resilience,
And the voice that helps us overcome.

It is the voice that speaks to us in our triumphs,
The voice that celebrates our victories,
The voice that reminds us of our power,
And the voice that helps us soar.

It is the voice that speaks to us in our relationships,
The voice that tells us to love and be loved,
The voice that reminds us of our connections,
And the voice that helps us build community.

It is the voice that speaks to us in our creativity,
The voice that tells us to express ourselves,
The voice that reminds us of our uniqueness,
And the voice that helps us create.

It is the voice that speaks to us in our spirituality,
The voice that tells us to seek the divine,
The voice that reminds us of our purpose,
And the voice that helps us find meaning.

The voice within is a powerful force,
A source of strength and wisdom,
A guide through the ups and downs of life,
And a reminder of our true selves.

So listen closely to the voice within,
And let it guide you on your journey,
For it is the voice of your soul,
And the voice of your truest self.

Jessie Z
Dulwich College Shanghai Puxi

The Voices In My Head

Take the chocolate!
Don't! Think of your brother!
He'll get another!
No! There's only one!
These are the voices in my head
An endless battle in my mind telling me to
Do this! Do that!
Why?
I yell back
Why must I listen to you?
Always telling me what to do
Why can't you leave me be!

This isn't good enough!
It's excellent!
No it isn't!
Be quiet won't you!
These are the voices in my head
Always squabbling
Forever yelling
It's not fair!
I scream at them
Just go away!

In the end though,
I suppose without the voices
My mind would be a void
Desolate and empty
Cold and dark

So I suppose I do want them to stay
For now at least...

Michelle B
Dulwich College Shanghai Puxi

The Wolves and the Phantoms

I
When the moon was tossed like a ball upon the trees,
The mist still grew on the blackened seas,
There will always be a shadow on a cliff so steep
The shadow of a wolf, and there an army sleep.

II
The wolf howled and bared its teeth,
Summoning its army for an attack in beneath,
Those army are still very organized
For they're preparing for attack, disguised.
They're so jealous of the richness of the castle
That they will risk their lives to come and hustle.

III
In the castle a feast is going
People are already dancing and cheering
No one noticed some strange things happening.
While the wolves shifted like they're the king.

IV
Still in the castle people danced,
They drank, they ate, and they glanced,
Out the window came the shadows,
Prepared and ready for the attack.

V
The leader wolf howled of the ultimate charge,

And the people inside saw the army – it's large,
The wolves they finally burst into the door,
With such force they're like an army of some boars.

VI
The people suddenly noticed something violent,
The music stopped and people fell silent
There was a long pause – a very long pause,
And the wolves, they charged and opened their jaws.

VII
The fight goes on, and the wolves started to bite,
But they realized one thing – those people are sprites
No, not really sprites, they're some phantom,
And they're here to celebrate once per annum.

VIII
A crow croaked on an old, dead tree,
A sound that makes hearts whizz like bees.
The wolves are now trampling, escaping and fleeing,
Because they can't beat the phantoms, who are already raging.

IX
The wolves are chased and never come back,
The party goes on, like nothing had happened,
And those wolves have finally learnt a lesson:
Never go rob or you'll be sent to heaven.

X
The sun finally comes after all,

Rolling into the sky like a round, red ball,
Those living things, they sang and cheered
And all goes well with a cup of good beer.

Ryan Z
Dulwich College Shanghai Pudong

To Me

To me you are the finest fruit I would find,
And you're the phenomenon that will stay in my mind forever.
To me you're the fragrance of happiness, laughter and joy,
You're the sound that brings me relaxation.
To me you're the person who spends time caring for me,
And you're the person I want to be able to live forever.
To me you are my golden trophy I can hold up proudly and confidently,
And you are my armor that protects me from the monsters in my life.
To me you are the strong chain painted with gold, holding everything together,
But best of all, you're my mom.

Julian
Dulwich College Shanghai Pudong

Untitled

The world built by concrete and steel bars
Listen to noisy people roaring in loud, boring cars
In this game of right and money, it's like life behind bars
A fast pace so annoying, it's tearing people apart
Relax my dear, just be silent and look up at the stars.

Ella
Dehong Shanghai International Chinese School

Villains

Hi, I'm homework
I am intelligent, brilliant and knowledgeable.
I am not like other villains
They are not smart and powerful
For example Miss Trunchbull isn't smart
And why would the yew tree stay in Conor?
Why can't Medusa look at a mirror?
Why does Joker live in hospital
And why does Voldemort look so ugly?
Why is Gothel super old?
Why is the ghost already dead?
Why does Bowser have a blind point?
Why does Taotie eat his body?
And that's why they can't defeat me!
Here are my abilities:
I can make depression
I can make aggression
With 3000 homeworks per day
Always writing essays
Having every week miserable
With horrible detention
With your parents talking with teachers
With your unbearable pain
You will carry your life with pain
With no happiness in life
You will carry your life with pain
Oh, how horrible is life?
With arguments with your mother and father
Carrying your pain and suffering

Go to the hell with your despondent heart
You will never be free with your restricted thoughts.

Gabriel L. Johnson S and Delon Z
Dulwich College Shanghai Puxi

Voice

Voices in my mind, soft and loud,
Whispers of doubt, fears that crowd.
Some calm, like morning breeze,
Others fierce, like stormy seas.

Dreams and hopes they all renew,
In the quiet space where thoughts accrue.

Amidst the noise, a gentle sound,
Speaking truths, always around.

Listening to the voices within,
They tell where I've been.
In life's chorus, let my voice be found,
A symphony of self, profound and sound.

Guiding me through paths unknown,
In the echo of my own.

Guiding me through paths unknown,
In the echo of my own.

Sam W
Dulwich International High School Programme Hengqin

Voice

Today, I heard a lovely and soft voice,
A voice I have never heard before in my life.
When I heard you call my name for the first time
In that lovely and soft voice
It made me feel like flying on a unicorn,
Sliding down the glimmering rainbow.
I wished to listen to your voice all day.

When I could no longer hear your calming voice again,
I prayed that I would hear that lovely voice one more time.
I felt like a rain-soaked blanket.
The world is so different without your voice.
Oh, how I miss your musical voice!

Shivika
Dulwich College Seoul

Voice of Silence

Silent, not a word.
It conveys thought, expression, and touch of heart.
It's a voice of love, but we might hurt.

This is the voice of a parent, waiting for her baby to sleep,
This is the voice of a couple, swapping souls deep,
This is the voice of a student, sitting in silence,
This is the voice of a teacher, leading with patience.

This is the voice of the Earth, whispering through the cave.
This is the voice of the supernova, illuminating the live.
This is the voice of the galaxy, bleak and quiet.
This is the voice of peace, that we all require.

Then listen carefully to the silent voice,
It's louder than any noise.
It's the voice of tomorrow, that never dies,
But it's the voice of a pledge, that always lies.

We find our way in the silence
To the brighter future, exploit the sense.
So let the silent voice orient you
For it's the voice to spread love to you.

Chonwai C
Dulwich International High School Programme Hengqin

Voice Poem

When I am with my friends, my voice is a flat whole eight note C.
When I am arguing with my brother, my voice is a barbarian husky.
It is inhale and howling when I stub my toe,
And low whimper when I am nervous.
When I am older my voice will be like an old witch,
I will use it to curse somebody I don't like.

Elaine H
Dulwich International High School Programme Hengqin

Voice Poem

When I am with my friends, my voice is a crazy clown.
When I am arguing with my sister, my voice is a noisy elephant.
It is a crying fish when I stub my toe,
And shivering cat when I am nervous.
When I am older my voice will be a calm tree.
I will use it to be a burning candle.

Joanna S
Dulwich International High School Programme Hengqin

Voices

There are voices all around us,
Voices of children chattering,
Voices of parents scolding,
Voices of teachers lecturing,
And even voices of animals talking to one another.

These voices are important,
Every voice should be heard.
Imagine a world with no voices,
No one can express their opinion.
Everywhere will be too quiet.

So let's start to express our thoughts,
And listen to people's opinions.
So there will be a purpose to our voices.

Emily K
Dulwich College Seoul

Voices

The 'v' stands for vulnerable, floating over the endless sea.
The 'o' stands for overlooked because some were destined to be.
The 'i' stands for invisible, trapped forever, never to be free.
The 'c' stands for caring because a mum's is gentle and soothing, that's a guarantee.
The 'e' stands for erasable because that's how insignificant it is and always will be.
The 's' stands for sardonic because some people misuse it, giving them pleasure, giving them glee.

But there really is only one word to describe a voice
And that is 'invaluable'
At least mine is.
They say it doesn't matter how big or small
But that's not true
And no one can prove me wrong.

Aparajita D
Dulwich College Seoul

Voices of People

In the symphony of life, your voice unfolds,
A melody of moments, both young and old.
Important echoes whisper through the years,
A lullaby of accomplishment, a symphony of tears.
Frustration weaves its thread within your song,
A tempest of emotions where resilience is strong.
Yet in the dissonance, a resilient tone,
For every challenge faced, a strength has grown.
Memories linger, like notes in the air,
A chorus of laughter, a speech of despair.
Your voice, a canvas painted with life's colors,
A mural of experience, both win and lose.
From the first tender cry to the words you now speak,
A journey through time, both bold and meek.
So let your voice resonate, a tale to be told,
A sonnet of existence, a ballad bold.

Taehui L
Dulwich College Seoul

Words

You can lose weight but you can't lose words.
You can't unsee what you've seen or unhear what you've heard,
'cause bad memories have never asked for permission.
You can lose people but won't ever forget them,
they'll live under your skin, even when you don't want them.
Yes you can forgive but you'll never forget,
'cause you can unfold the paper but it's gonna stay bent.

So it really is something deeply deranged,
commenting on something another can't change.
How entitled of you
to think you get a say.

They will lose weight,
but they'll never lose those words.

Caroline L
Dulwich College Shanghai Pudong

You Are...

To me, you are a bowl of hot noodles because your hugs give me a warm sensation,
You are a bright path that guides me through life,
You are the scent of an amazing salmon sandwich,
And you are the sound of ten thousand orchestras cheering me on.
You are the morning ride that took me to the bread shop,
And a journey through the mountain roads in a Miata.
You are my piano gold medal,
You are the shelter protecting me from dangers,
You are the brightest star in my life.
But best of all, you are my dad.
Thank you.

Alexander Y
Dulwich College Shanghai Pudong

www.ingramcontent.com/pod-product-compliance
Lightning Source LLC
Chambersburg PA
CBHW040732220426
43209CB00087B/1593